W9-BCX-952

DATE DUE

HOCKEY
FOR FUN!

By Sandra Will

Content Adviser: Jim Bugenhagen, Director of Hockey, Chelsea Piers–Sky Rink, New York, New York
Reading Adviser: Frances J. Bonacci, Reading Specialist, Cambridge, Massachusetts

COMPASS POINT BOOKS
MINNEAPOLIS, MINNESOTA

Compass Point Books
3109 West 50th Street, #115
Minneapolis, MN 55410

Visit Compass Point Books on the Internet at *www.compasspointbooks.com*
or e-mail your request to *custserv@compasspointbooks.com*

Photographs ©: Rubberball, front cover (left); Artville, front cover (right), back cover, 5; Getty Royalty Free, front cover (background), 14–15, 42 (top center), 42 (top right), 43 (top left); Corel, 4, 8, 12, 42 (center left), 44, 45 (bottom right), 47; Mitchell Layton/Getty Images, 6–7, 9; Robert Leberge/Getty Images, 10–11, 16–17; Courtesy of The Hockey Company, 13 (top left), 13 (bottom right), 43 (bottom left); Courtesy of Easton, 13 (center top), 13 (center bottom), 13 (bottom left), 45 (top right); Doug Pensinger/Getty Images, 19; Brian Bahr/Getty Images, 21, 33, 37, 43 (bottom center); Todd Warshaw/Getty Images, 23; Doug Sandford/Getty Images, 24–25; Mike Powell/Getty , 26–27; Harry How/Getty Images, 28–29; Jeff Vinnick/Getty Images, 30; Al Bello/Getty Images, 34–35; Hulton Archive/Getty Images, 38; 42 (center right); Rick Stewart/Getty Images, 39; Elsa/Getty Images, 41

Editor: Elizabeth Bond/Bill SMITH STUDIO
Photo Researchers: Sandra Will, Sean Livingstone, and Christie Silver/Bill SMITH STUDIO
Designer: Colleen Sweet/Bill SMITH STUDIO

Library of Congress Cataloging-in-Publication Data
Will, Sandra.
    Hockey for fun! / by Sandra Will.
    p. cm. — (Sports for fun!)
    Summary: Describes the sport of hockey and presents information on the
    basic equipment, different moves, scoring, rules and more.
    Includes bibliographical references (p.) and index.
    ISBN 0-7565-0488-0 (hardcover : alk. paper)
    1. Hockey—Juvenile literature. [1. Hockey.] I. Title. II. Series.
    GV847.25.W55 2004
    796.962—dc21
                                2003006674

Table of Contents

Note: In this book, there are two kinds of vocabulary words. Hockey Words to Know are words specific to hockey. They are in **bold** and are defined on page 46. Other Words to Know are helpful words that aren't related only to hockey. They are in ***bold and italicized.*** These are defined on page 47.

Winter Is for Hockey!

Have you ever imagined flying across the ice? Every winter, people of all ages lace up a pair of skates and play hockey on frozen ponds, lakes, and in indoor arenas. The game of hockey traces its roots back hundreds of years, but no one knows for sure who invented the game of hockey or when it was first played. The sport made its way to North America during the 19th century. Canadians are credited with turning hockey into the game we know and love today.

Goal of the Game

Hockey is a team sport. The object of the game is to score more **goals,** or points, than the other team. A team scores goals by shooting the puck into the other team's net. A **goaltender,** or goalie, tries to stop the puck from entering the net.

A hockey puck weighs about 6 ounces (170 grams). It is 1 inch (2.5 centimeters) thick and 3 inches (8 cm) wide. Hockey pucks are made of vulcanized, or toughened, rubber.

On the Ice

American hockey rinks measure 200 feet (61 meters) long and 85 feet (26 meters) wide. International hockey rinks are 15 feet (5 m) wider, totaling 100 feet (31 m). **Protective** boards made of fiberglass surround the rink and stand 40 to 48 inches (102 to 122 cm) in height. **Synthetic** glass is attached to the boards and protects the crowd from flying pucks. Blue and red lines extend across the width of the rink and divide the playing surface into zones. Look at the picture to learn the names of the parts of the hockey rink.

goal

goal line

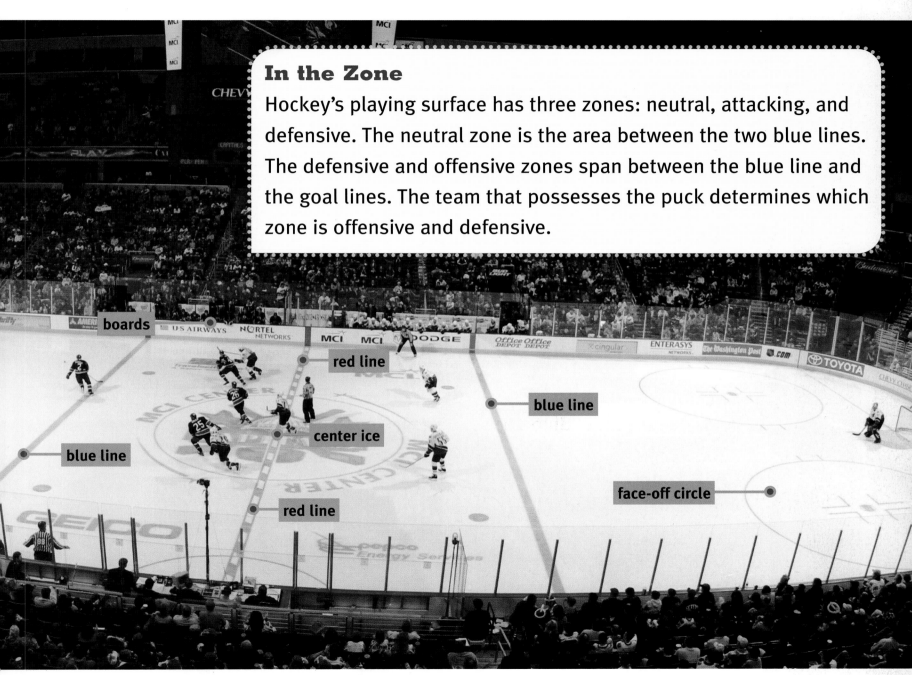

In the Zone

Hockey's playing surface has three zones: neutral, attacking, and defensive. The neutral zone is the area between the two blue lines. The defensive and offensive zones span between the blue line and the goal lines. The team that possesses the puck determines which zone is offensive and defensive.

boards

red line

blue line

center ice

blue line

face-off circle

red line

The Roster

Each team has five **_position_** players and one goaltender on the ice. Before each game, the coach prepares a roster for the game. The roster lists the players who are **_eligible_** to play during the game. Coaches can have up to 18 players and two goalies on each game roster.

Players sit on the bench while they wait to enter the game. Skaters can enter the game from the bench without stopping the game. This is known as "changing on the fly." Players jump over the boards in front of the bench to enter the game in a hurry. Coaches often send in a whole group of players at one time, which is called a line change.

Players sitting on the bench must pay close attention to the game. They must be ready to enter the game at a moment's notice!

Beware!

When changing players on the fly, the player leaving the ice must be within five feet of the bench before the **substitute** player enters the game, or the player earns a penalty.

Slap It In!

It's game time! A hockey game is divided into three 20-minute **periods.** Every period of play is separated by a 15-minute **intermission.** During each period, teams try to score more goals than their **opponent.** Players can only score goals one way in hockey. They must shoot the puck over the red goal line, between the goalposts, and into the opposing team's net. To score a goal, shooters must be able to beat the opponent's goalie and slap the puck into the net.

What's the Score?

Sometimes it is difficult to tell if the puck crosses the goal line and enters the net. A **goal judge** sits behind each team's goal (off the ice) and decides whether a shot scores. The judge uses a special machine behind the net to signal goals. When a team scores, a red light flashes!

Canadian goaltender Kim St. Pierre watches as the puck enters the net during the 2002 Winter Olympics. Canada defeated the United States in the women's final to win the gold medal.

Suit Up

Imagine a frozen puck traveling more than 100 miles (161 km) per hour at your head! Hockey requires special equipment that protects players and helps them play the game.

Each player wears a jersey (called a sweater) and pants over his or her hockey gear. Hockey pants have pads that cover the hips, thighs, and tailbone.

Hockey sticks are all the same shape. Sticks are made of wood, **aluminum,** or other materials. Players also use sticks with different amounts of flex, or **bend.**

A hard plastic helmet protects a player's head from injury. Many players (such as the boy pictured at left) choose to wear a face mask and plastic visor for additional protection.

Players wear shoulder, elbow, and shin pads to protect them from sticks, pucks, and **collisions.**

Skates with metal blades allow players to "fly" across the ice. Originally made of leather, skates come in a **variety** of materials and styles.

Gloves help guard a player's hands and wrists from injury.

Get in Goal

Goalies wear a mask and leg guards to shield them from flying pucks and collisions in front of the net. Special gloves called catchers and blockers help goalies block shots and catch the puck.

leg guards

mask

catcher

blocker

Start It Up!

Each game begins with a **face-off** at center ice. The centers from each team stand one stick-width apart from each other, facing the opponent's goalie. The **referee** blows his whistle and drops the puck between the players' sticks. Both centers battle for the puck and try to gain *possession* for their team. Referees hold center face-offs after each goal is scored and to begin each period.

In Your Face!

A hockey rink has a total of five face-off circles: one at center ice and two in each defensive zone. Referees and **linesmen** hold face-offs in all five circles to resume play after they stop the game for a *violation.*

On the Attack

The **offense** is responsible for moving the puck into the attacking zone and scoring. Hockey has two types of offensive positions:

Center: The center acts as the team's quarterback. A center directs the play of the game in both the offensive and defensive zones. Centers must be good at face-offs and be able to pass and shoot well.

Wings: The wings, also known as forwards, play on each side of the center. They move up and down the ice, exchanging passes with the center. On offense, the wings try to shoot goals and make **rebounds.** On **defense,** they guard the opponent's wings. There are two wing players—the left wing and the right wing. The left wing plays mostly on the left side of the ice, and the right wing covers the right side of the rink.

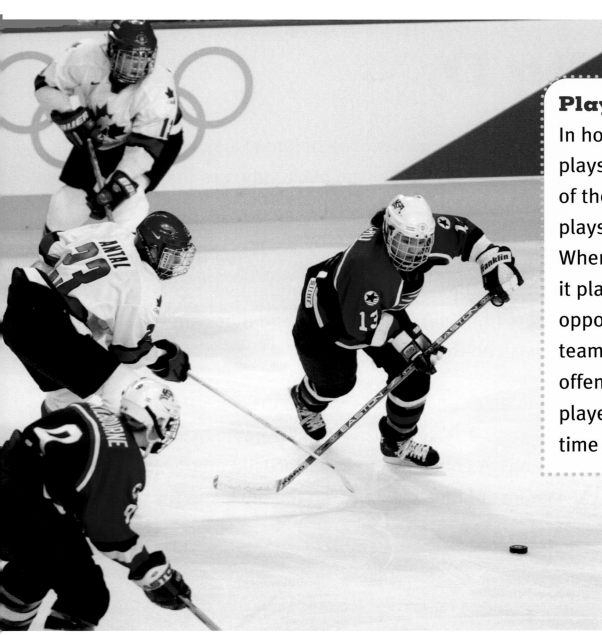

Playing Both Ways

In hockey, the offense also plays defense. Possession of the puck determines who plays offense and defense. When a team has the puck, it plays offense. If the opponent has the puck, a team plays defense. Both offensive and defensive players can score at any time during the game.

U.S. forward Julie Chu chases down the puck while being pressured by opposing players.

The Big D

A strong defense wins hockey games. The defense keeps the opponent's offense from scoring and gains control of the puck. Here are the two defensive positions:

Defensemen: Each team has two defensemen—one on the right side and one on the left side. They defend their end of the ice and prevent goals. Defensemen clear players from in front of the net and block shots. On offense, defensemen pass the puck up the ice.

Goaltender: The goaltender, or goalie, tries to stop the puck from entering the net. Goalies must have good *agility,* so they can scramble in front of the net with all of their equipment. A goalie has to keep focused on the events of the game. They are the last line of defense between the puck and the goal.

Goaltender Martin Brodeur (#30) of the New Jersey Devils makes a glove save against the Carolina Hurricanes. The Devils defeated the Hurricanes 3–1.

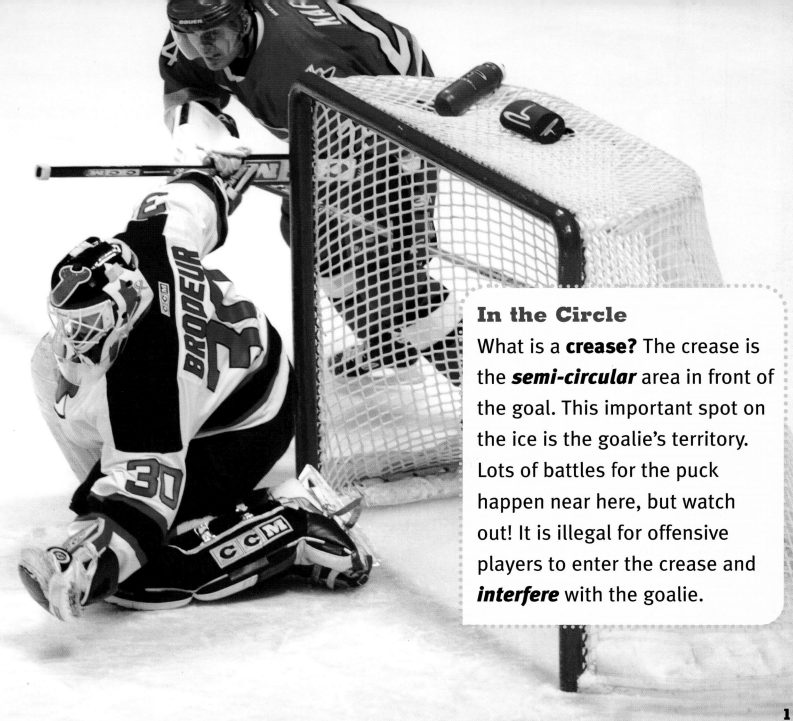

In the Circle

What is a **crease?** The crease is the *semi-circular* area in front of the goal. This important spot on the ice is the goalie's territory. Lots of battles for the puck happen near here, but watch out! It is illegal for offensive players to enter the crease and *interfere* with the goalie.

Forward Motion

Passing makes hockey a team game. Players pass the puck to each other and try to move the puck into scoring position. A good pass can beat more than one defenseman. Two or three good passes often lead to a goal. The last player to pass the puck to the goal scorer earns an **assist.**

Keep passes short. Long passes tend to be cut off by opposing players. Different types of passes are helpful in many game situations. There are four kinds of passes in hockey. Try practicing each one.

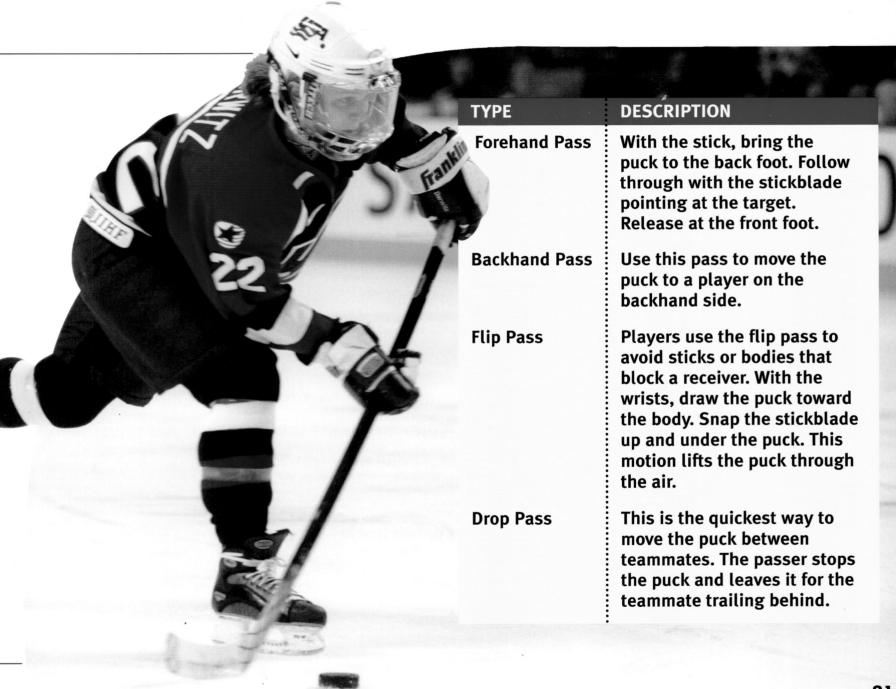

TYPE	DESCRIPTION
Forehand Pass	With the stick, bring the puck to the back foot. Follow through with the stickblade pointing at the target. Release at the front foot.
Backhand Pass	Use this pass to move the puck to a player on the backhand side.
Flip Pass	Players use the flip pass to avoid sticks or bodies that block a receiver. With the wrists, draw the puck toward the body. Snap the stickblade up and under the puck. This motion lifts the puck through the air.
Drop Pass	This is the quickest way to move the puck between teammates. The passer stops the puck and leaves it for the teammate trailing behind.

Take a Shot!

How do players beat the opposing goalie and score? Goal scorers see the puck and look for ways to slip the puck into the net. Players often use different types of shots to find "open holes," or weak spots, in the net past the goalie.

- Wrist Shot: An all-purpose, hard, and accurate shot. Players can use a wrist shot while standing still or skating fast.

- Backhand Shot: Most players consider the backhand shot their secret weapon. The backhand motion tells the goalie that the puck will travel high. Shooters who keep the backhand shot low fool the goalie and score many goals.

- Slap Shot: The most powerful shot in hockey. The slap shot is a great way to score but hard to control. Players use a full-body windup to launch the puck at the net.

• Snap Shot: The quickest way to score. The snap shot is a combination of the wrist and slap shots. The shot requires almost no windup, so the shooter has the element of surprise. Since the goalies have no warning, it is the toughest shot for them to stop.

Tip Your Hat
When a player scores three goals in one game, it is called a **hat trick**!

Accuracy is an important part of shooting and scoring. Wayne Gretzky was one of the most accurate scorers in NHL history.

The Enforcers

How does the defense stop the offense? It checks, or hits, its opponent. Players use their bodies to gain possession of the puck. Checking allows defensive players to move the offense out of position. The proper use of checking is a very good way to disrupt offensive attacks and prevent goals. Some players are used in the game especially for their checking skills. Hockey fans have a special name for checkers: "the enforcers."

Right wing Marty McInnis (#10) of the Boston Bruins checks defenseman Robert Svehla (#67) of the Toronto Maple Leafs against the boards during an NHL game.

Use Your Body

Checking makes hockey a collision sport. **Full-body checks** send players crashing into the boards or flying across the ice. But not all checks involve colliding bodies. Defenders often "poke" the puck away from their opponents with their sticks. This is known as a **poke-check** or **stick-check.** Goalies sometimes use stick-checks to protect the net from players coming around the backside of the goal.

False Moves

Is a **deke** named after a guy who played hockey? No. Deke comes from the word "decoy," which is something used to lure someone into a trap.

Players in possession of the puck use dekes to get around an opponent. Here's how it works. The player who has the puck draws defenders. Using the puck as bait, a player fakes out opponents and beats the defenders. The puck handler is able to move the puck down the ice toward the goal without interference from defenders.

Dekes are also a good way to make the goalie move out of position, opening up the net for a score.

To deke, move the puck or your body to one side. Then move in the opposite direction.

Follow the Rules

Hockey is a game with many rules—93 to be exact! It would be difficult to learn all of them, but it is most important to learn as many rules as possible. Here are some of the rules:

• The puck must be kept in motion at all times.

• The puck may be passed between players who are in the same zone. The puck cannot be passed from a player in one zone to a player on the same team who is in another zone. If a team violates this rule, it is charged with being **offside.**

• The position of a player's skates determines whether he or she is offside. A player is offside when both skates are over the outer edge of the center or blue line involved in the play.

- Players of an attacking, or offensive, team may not enter the attacking zone before the puck. Violations of this rule result in a stoppage of play and a face-off.

- When both teams have all six players on the ice, a player cannot shoot the puck from his or her side of the red line across the opponent's goal line. This is known as **icing the puck.** When a team ices the puck, referees stop the game and hold a face-off in the defensive zone. A team that has fewer than six players can ice the puck without stopping the game.

Mario Lemieux of the Pittsburgh Penguins attempts to control a rolling puck and keep the puck in motion.

Safety First

Hockey is a high-speed, physical game. To protect players' safety, certain types of conduct are not allowed during the game. Here are a few of the many *illegal* moves in hockey:

Roughing: striking an opponent or committing rough behavior on the ice

Hooking: keeping players from making a play by "hooking" them with the stick

Charging: skating or jumping into an opponent

High sticking: any contact made with a stick above an opponent's shoulders

Interference: getting in the way of an opponent who does not have the puck

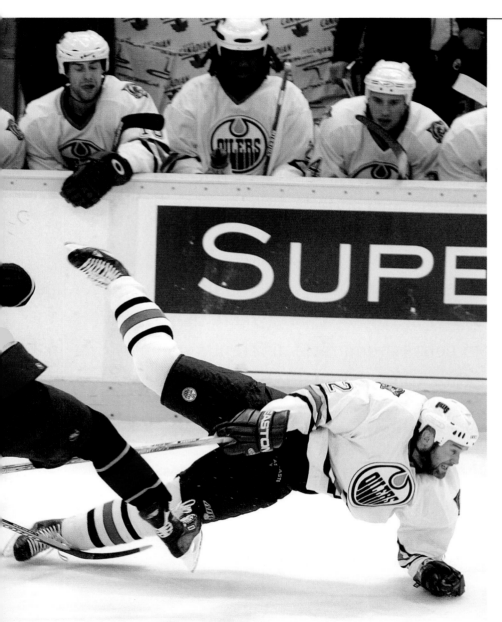

Checking from behind: hitting players from behind, preventing them from defending themselves

Kneeing: using a knee to interfere with an opponent

Give Me A "C"

Each team has a captain who wears a "C" on his or her jersey. Only the captain can speak with the referee about violations.

Alexander Frolov (#24) of the Los Angeles Kings trips his opponent, earning a penalty for kneeing.

In the Box

What happens when a player does something illegal during the game? The referee blows his whistle and gives the player a penalty. Hockey has three types of penalties: minor, major, and misconduct. Misconduct penalties are divided into basic, game, or gross.

The type of penalty called by the official depends on how badly the player has behaved. Referees send players to the **penalty box**, where they spend time for their punishment. Each type of penalty requires a different amount of time in the box. Here is some basic information on penalties:

TYPE	EXAMPLE OF OFFENSE	TIME IN PENALTY BOX
Minor	Roughing, slashing, tripping, holding, hooking	2 minutes
Major	Fighting, injuring an opponent	5 minutes
Misconduct (basic, game, or gross)	Yell at referee, cross-checking	10 minutes or thrown out of the game

Taking Advantage

To win hockey games more easily, teams must be able to score during a **power play.**

The referee just called a penalty on the opposing team and sent one of its players to the penalty box. During the penalty time, the opposing team cannot substitute another player. It must play with fewer skaters on the ice. So one team has an advantage on the ice during the penalty—this is called the power play. The power play lasts until the team with the advantage scores, or penalty time ends—whichever happens first.

During a power play, the penalized team hopes to **"kill" the penalty** by keeping the other team from scoring. It puts all its players on defense and tries to ice the puck to run time off the clock. And once in a while, the team with the disadvantage manages to score—it's a **shorthanded goal**!

Team USA celebrates a power play goal during its game against Canada. The two teams competed for the gold medal in the 2002 Winter Olympic Games. Team Canada won 5–2.

The Pros

North America has one major **_professional_** organization, known as the National Hockey League (NHL). The NHL is divided into two conferences, with a total of 30 teams: the Eastern Conference and the Western Conference. Canada is home to six NHL teams, and the other 24 teams are located in the United States.

Besides the pros, North America also has several minor and amateur leagues. Minor league hockey teams train young players and sometimes send players to the NHL. Canada has three leagues, known as the juniors. These three leagues make up the Canadian Hockey League (CHL). The CHL is considered to be the top feeder system for sending players to the NHL.

People in more than 50 countries play hockey. The International Ice Hockey Federation (IIHF) oversees hockey leagues across the world.

Girl Power!

Since the late 1800s, women have been playing hockey. But women's hockey was never widely played or popular until the 1990s. Today, women in more than 30 countries participate in amateur and professional hockey!

Legends

Thousands of players have contributed to hockey's amazing history. Gordie Howe and Wayne Gretzky are two of the game's best.

Gordie Howe

Many people consider Gordie Howe the greatest all-around hockey player of all time. He was born in Floral, Saskatchewan, on March 31, 1928. He played his first NHL game at age 18 for the Detroit Red Wings. Howe played 32 seasons in the NHL, spanning five decades. He holds the record for the most games ever played in the NHL: 1,767. During his career, he scored 801 goals and earned 1,049 assists. He was one of the top five scorers in the NHL for 20 **consecutive** seasons. Howe played until the incredible age of 52, retiring in 1980. Because of his abilities and achievements, Gordie Howe is known as "Mr. Hockey."

Wayne Gretzky

Wayne Gretzky is perhaps the most dominant hockey player ever to step on the ice. Born on January 26, 1961, in Brantford, Ontario, Gretzky began skating at age two. When he was only 10 years old, Gretzky scored 378 goals in one year! He joined the NHL at age 18 and won the Most Valuable Player (MVP) trophy during his rookie season. Gretzky went on to win the MVP trophy nine times in his career. During his 19 seasons in the NHL, he scored 894 goals and earned 1,963 assists. When he retired in 1999, Wayne Gretzky owned or shared 61 NHL records! For his unbelievable hockey talents, he is known as "The Great One."

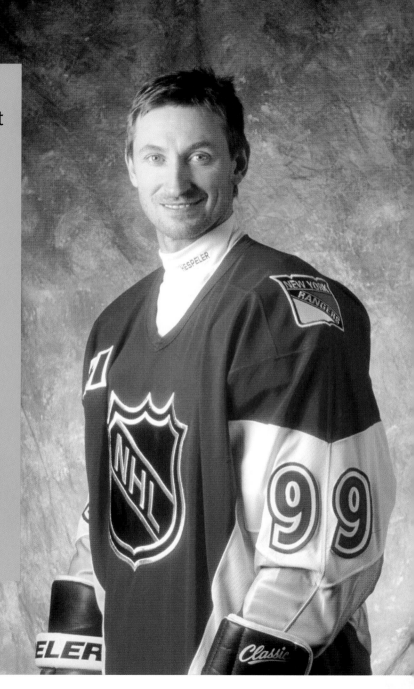

A Royal Legacy

The Stanley Cup has a rich history and is considered to be the finest trophy in all of sports. In 1892, Lord Stanley of Preston of England donated a silver and gold bowl to Canada. Originally, the trophy was given each year to the best Canadian amateur team.

In 1915, American hockey clubs were allowed to compete for the cup. Professional teams from many leagues battled for the honor. The Stanley Cup became the official championship of the NHL in 1926.

The Stanley Cup is a best-of-seven-games series that starts every year in late May. It pits the two teams against each other that have won the playoff rounds from the Eastern and Western Conferences. The first team to win four games is the champion of the NHL.

Stanley Cup Statistics

Several teams have dominated the Stanley Cup. Here are some of the teams with the most titles:

TEAM	TITLES
Montreal Canadiens	23
Toronto Maple Leafs	11
Detroit Red Wings	10
Edmonton Oilers	5
New York Rangers	4

Pavel Datsyuk of the Detroit Red Wings raises the Stanley Cup after winning the 2002 NHL championship. The Red Wings beat the Carolina Hurricanes in five games.

What Happened When?

1823 **1870** **1880** **1890** **1900** **1910** **1920** **1930** **1940**

Early 1800s Ice hockey makes its first appearance in Canada.

1877 The Montreal *Gazette* publishes the first known hockey rules.

1888 The Amateur Hockey Association of Canada is formed.

1892 The first women's hockey game is played in Canada.

1893 Lord Stanley of Preston, the English governor-general of Canada, donates a silver and gold trophy to Canada, which becomes the Stanley Cup.

1895 College athletes from the U.S. and Canada play the first international hockey games.

1910 The National Hockey Association is formed.

1912 The number of players allowed on the ice is reduced from seven to six per team.

1917 Four NHA teams reorganize to form the National Hockey League. The Seattle Metropolitans become the first American-based team to win the Stanley Cup.

1923 The first hockey game is broadcast on the radio.

1924 Ice hockey becomes a full medal sport at the Winter Olympic Games. Canada wins the gold medal.

1924 Canadian Men's Hockey Team

1946 Referees begin using hand signals to indicate penalties and other calls.

1950   **1960**   **1970**   **1980**   **1990**   **2000**

1949 The center red line first appears on the ice.

1952 Hockey Night makes its television debut in Canada.

1955 The Zamboni makes its first appearance in the NHL.

1957 CBS is the first U.S. television network to broadcast an NHL game.

1958 Willie O'Ree of the Boston Bruins becomes the first African-American player in the NHL.

1961 The Hockey Hall of Fame opens in Toronto.

1974 The USSR wins the first World Junior Hockey Championship.

1980 The U.S. men's hockey team defeats the best teams in the world to win the gold medal in the Winter Olympics. The victory is known as the "Miracle on Ice."

1994 The NHL has its first major labor dispute, and players miss games for 103 days. The regular season becomes the shortest in 53 years.

1994 Wayne Gretzky scores his 802nd career goal and breaks Gordie Howe's record.

1998 NHL players compete in the Olympics for the first time. Women's ice hockey becomes a full medal sport in the Winter Olympics. The U.S. wins the first gold medal.

2002 The Canadian men and women sweep the Winter Olympics, winning gold medals in both men's and women's hockey.

2002 Canadian Women's Hockey Team

43

Hockey Highlights

A Zamboni is a four-wheel-drive vehicle that scrapes, cleans, and washes the surface of the ice before each period. Frank Zamboni invented the machine in 1949.

Goaltenders wear colorful designs on their masks. Each goalie *customizes* his or her helmet, usually with their team's colors and logo.

Hockey players skate across the ice at speeds of up to 30 miles (48 km) per hour!

In 1990, the United States had about 5,500 registered women's hockey players. By the year 2000, there were more than six times as many registered women!

Teams "retire" jersey numbers to honor their best players. Once a number is retired, no other player can wear it.

Goaltender Glenn Hall played in 503 consecutive games—an NHL record. He played with Detroit and Chicago from October 1955 through November 1962.

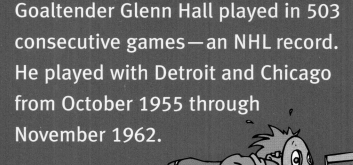

The New York Islanders are the only team in NHL history to win 19 consecutive playoff series.

Hockey Words to Know

assist: when a player helps set up the goal by passing the puck to the goalscorer

bend: the amount that a stickblade will give or curve

crease: the semi-circular area in front of the goal

defense: when the team tries to stop the offense from scoring

deke: a fake by a player with the puck to get around an opponent or the goalie

face-off: the action of an official dropping the puck between the sticks of two opposing players to start play

full-body check: using your entire body to bump an opposing player

goal: a point scored; also the netted area into which the puck must land for a goal to be scored

goal judge: the official who sits behind the goalie and signals a goal with a red light

goaltender: the player who guards the net and keeps the puck from entering the goal; also known as goalie

hat trick: three goals scored by one player in one game

icing the puck: when a player shoots the puck from his or her side of the red line across the opponent's goal line

infraction: a violation of the rules

"kill" the penalty: when a penalized team keeps the opponent from scoring during a power play

linesmen: the officials who call offside and icing and handle all face-offs in the defensive zones

offense: when the team has the puck and tries to score goals

offside: when a player crosses the attacking zone blue line before the puck does

passing: moving the puck between players

penalty: a punishment for breaking the rules

penalty box: the area where players serve their penalty time

period: one 20-minute session in a hockey game

poke-check: see stick-check

power play: when a team has more players on the ice than the opposing team, because of one or more penalties against the opposing team

rebound: a missed shot that bounces off the goal or boards

referee: the official who calls the penalties and handles the face-offs at center ice

shorthanded goal: when a penalized team scores during the other team's power play

stick-check: when a player uses his or her stick to take the puck away from an opponent

Metric Conversion
1 yard = .9144 meters

Other Words to Know

Here are definitions for some of the words used in this book:

accuracy: free from mistakes or errors

agility: quick and easy movement

aluminum: a type of metal

collision: when two things run into each other

consecutive: in a row, without stopping

customize: to make personal

eligible: able to do something

illegal: against the rules

interfere: to get in the way of an opponent

intermission: a break between periods of activity

opponent: the other team, or a player on the other team

position: where the player stands and what the player is supposed to do

possession: when a team controls the puck

professional: a person paid to do a job or play a game

protective: something that makes you more safe so you don't get hurt

semi-circular: half of a circle

substitute: a person or thing that replaces another person or thing

synthetic: not real, fake

variety: many different kinds

violation: breaking a rule

Where To Learn More

AT THE LIBRARY

Ayers, Tom. *The Illustrated Rules of Ice Hockey*. Carmel, NY: Ideals Publications, 2001.

Kramer, Sydelle A. *Hockey's Greatest Players*. New York: Random House, Inc., 1999.

Sias, John. *Kids' Book of Hockey: Skills, Strategies, Equipment, and the Rules of the Game*. New York: Carol Publishing Group, 1997.

ON THE ROAD

Hockey Hall of Fame

BCE Place
30 Yonge Street
Toronto, Ontario
Canada M5E 1X8
416/360-7765
http://www.hhhof.com

United States Hockey Hall of Fame

801 Hat Trick Avenue
Eveleth, MN 55734
218/744-5167
http://www.ushockeyhall.com

ON THE WEB

For more information on hockey, use FactHound to track down Web sites related to this book.

1. Go to *www.facthound.com*
2. Type in this book ID: 0756504880
3. Click on the *FETCH IT* button.

Your trusty FactHound will fetch the best Web sites for you!

INDEX

ABOUT THE AUTHOR

Sandra Will graduated magna cum laude from Barnard College, Columbia University, with a B.A. degree in English Literature. Sandra's passion for sports stems from her childhood. When she is not watching a game, she enjoys reading books, visiting museums, and playing with her dog, Maggie. Originally from Chehalis, Washington, Sandra lives in New York City.